Suicide

BY DEREK O'NEILL

DEDICATION

To all who read this book, I salute you for wanting to change the way you live for the better and for having the courage to be who you are as fully as possible.

To all who encourage me everyday to keep going and sharing their lives with me, family small and large. But most of all the little angels who came to teach me – Alexa and Blake, my grandchildren.

"Everybody hurts sometimes, and when we do it is nice to have Derek O'Neill around. His excellent little books on the things that get us, (fear, anger, depression, victimhood, mental blocks) allow us to find our way safely through our psychological minefields and arrive safely at the other side. Read them when you need them."

Paul Perry, Author of the
New York Times Bestseller
Evidence of the Afterlife

TABLE OF CONTENTS

AUTHOR'S PREFACE

Thank you for purchasing *Suicide – Fast or Slow.* This book has not come about as a result of my training as a therapist, but through some hard-earned lessons that I have experienced myself. This is how I know the path out of limiting beliefs and behaviors that hinder growth. The tools that I offer in this book have worked not only for me, but also for hundreds if not thousands of other people. I have shared these ideas and techniques in my workshops, one-on-one sessions, video and radio broadcasts, and on my website, and I have witnessed astounding results time and time again. Through observation of others, and myself, I have learned to identify the triggers and root causes of disharmony. Most of all, I have come to understand and apply the best methods for achieving peace and balance in life; not perfection, but real transformation and harmony that comes with learning who we are and what makes us tick. My 35 years of martial arts study has given me a refined sense of timing for when to strike with the sword to cut away old patterns, and when to use the brush to paint the picture of the life we deserve and can have.

The 'Get a Grip' series of books offers tangible, authentic wisdom that can help you in all aspects of your life. You've made a great choice by investing in this book. Enjoy the read, and take time to learn and apply the techniques. Let's change who we are together.

Derek

Suicide
Fast or Slow

TALKING ABOUT SUICIDE; A HEALING PERSPECTIVE

Suicide knows no boundaries or limitations. It affects people from every segment of society. The problems and challenges a person is struggling with can be obvious, however sometimes they are not. Suicidal thoughts arise from the feeling that there is no other option to stop the pain. There is a loss of perspective. The mind creates a false reality that sees "ending it all" as the only alternative. Suicide is often not the wish to die, but rather a way to cease unbearable agony or anguish.

The news that someone has died from suicide, whether we personally knew them or not, is tragic and frustrating. Making sense of this kind of death is extremely difficult. It's essential that we all educate ourselves about every aspect of suicide – the risk factors, prevention, the behaviors that are signs and warnings, and how to cope when someone has died. Both as someone who may be in a deep depression, or as a friend or family member of someone afflicted, we can to try to put it into perspective, find hope, and at the very least, recognize when a problem has moved beyond something we can handle on our own.

Whether you are looking for tools to help someone close to you, or you yourself are grappling with very dark feelings that veer toward suicidal thoughts, there is valuable and practical information in the pages that follow. Though a tough subject, learning about suicide can lead to both practical, life-saving actions, and deeper understanding of how someone can reach the point of thinking there are no options (in reality, there ALWAYS are.) Most people who die by suicide wanted to find an alternative, but felt they could not. Leading up to suicide, whether it is sudden, or the slow-evolving kind, self-destructive behavior and attitudes become addictive, increasing the inability to see beyond the false beliefs and solutions. This is when people enter what I call "the dark night of the soul."

When someone has given up on experiencing life, and is looking for an escape from the pain they associate with it, dying by their own hand makes sense to them. Usually they also convince themselves that people in their lives are better off without them. Though the exact opposite is true, in reality we have to understand that the suicidal person's mindset has become their reality.

In the vast majority of suicide cases, there was a treatable mental disorder, with depression as the most common factor.

Many times the condition was undiagnosed. Environmental factors and conditions (physical illness, financial problems, a tragic loss, etc.) can play a role. In a smaller, yet still significant percentage of suicide victims, there was no sign or warning, which is especially shocking and confusing as we try to understand the mysterious "why." Sometimes coming out of a depression can be more of a risk for suicide than being in the middle of a deep despair. The fear of sinking back into depression becomes the trigger, which we will learn more about in the next section.

Most of us have, or will be, affected by suicide to varying degrees - either through the loss of someone we know, or by helping a friend or family member who has experienced the suicide of a person dear to them. The severe and complicated experience of losing a loved one to suicide can last a lifetime. A family may feel the effects for generations. Many people are dealing with deep depression or seemingly unsolvable problems that paint their lives as hopeless. You might suffer from these feelings. Remember, there is help, no matter which of these situations has brought you here.

It is so important to be genuine when it comes to the subject of suicide. If you feel you are in a destructive state of mind, be honest with yourself and accept that you will find a way to come out of crisis. If you are trying to help someone else, speak to them from your heart. You have to be as genuine with them as you possibly can. How can you express "I know how you feel," if you've never been severely depressed or suicidal? Giving that person hope in a genuinely compassionate and concerned way is better. You can tell them, "I love you and want to help you. Let me call a counselor for you."

UNDERSTANDING AND RETHINKING THE ELEMENTS OF SUICIDE

I have studied suicide for decades, and worked with many suicidal people and their families. There are aspects of what happens when someone is suicidal that we need to re-educate ourselves about.

The signs that someone is suicidal are usually obvious, but we often don't see them. We all know that severe depression can lead to suicide. It is common that someone can be slowly but steadily coming out of a depression or heightened state of anxiety when they suddenly hit a glitch, or an ice patch, so to speak, and begin to slide into a negative pattern of thinking. Those thoughts can become so dark that they don't feel there is a way out of them. The mind begins to look for anything to hold on to. They, along with friends and family, don't realize what is going on, but it can lead to suicide about three days later. Afterwards, you'll hear statements like, "you're joking, I was only talking to him yesterday, he never seemed as happy."

A person emerging from depression can become so overwhelmed and panicked with the terror that they could be going back into that black hole. A stressful event can also trigger the slide. Their mind clicks and they actually began to find calm, peace, and happiness in the decision that they are going to kill themselves. Thoughts of bliss overtake the fear of dying. We need to learn about this critical series of events and see the signs. Usually, everybody is looking for the opposite – an obvious worsening of symptoms, but about three days before a suicide a sudden calm can be an urgent warning.

We can only guess what thoughts go through the mind of someone who attempts - or carries out – a suicide. Do they think of what they will leave behind? I'm sure the part of the brain that would usually be focused on that shuts down at some point. It is reasonable to assume that they love us and would not consider suicide if they had something to hold onto. People who are able to stop themselves seem to gain access to the place in the brain where the acceptance and bliss are stored that prevent suicide. I would love neuroscientists to test this theory. I've seen the mind change people physically, as well as mentally. I believe if we study this, we would gain insights into how we might be able to trigger a part of the mind that's locked down by a word, a set of words, or a gesture, and if so, we might start saving lives.

We live in a changing world. Acceptance and tolerance is growing across many societies and yet so many people are still coping with cultural ideas of what "should be," as well as external influences of what roles are expected of us. When people find themselves at odds with these conflicting beliefs, they can lose confidence and slide into self-destruction. Sometimes it's family pressures. I'll never forget the doctor who came to see me who had attempted suicide many times. He was addicted to his own medication. His father was a prominent heart surgeon and his mother was another specialist. From an early age he was pushed into being a doctor, even though he had wanted to be a painter. He lived most of his life as an extremely sad person who was not living his own genuine path.

Another area of concern that suicide is sometimes a consequence of, is the struggle many young people are having over gender and sexual identity. Again, we see changes, but boys, especially, are coming up against ideas of what is manly and "macho." To be gentle, softer, and kind is discouraged. I see teens and young men turning to Ecstasy or "E-tablets," which triggers the brain in a way that allows them to be affectionate and tender with one another. The excessive drinking of water under the influence of E-tablets embodies the symbol of purification and renewal. We need to be aware of how cultures, groups, and families can create limiting ideas and thoughts about identity and individuality. As young people set out to "find themselves," let's be more sensitive and responsible to their needs to be accepted and supported.

Self-destructive behavior that persists is often "slow suicide." Using substances or severely neglecting one's health can be a path to eventual death for some people, especially with long term alcohol and/or drug abuse. Even a smoker, knowing that they are surely going to kill themselves in the end, must face the fact they are trading instant gratification for a full life. Many people are eating their way to an early grave.

Looking at what the emotions and history are behind the self-destruction, and getting help - for both critical situations and for protracted behavior - is so important. Compulsion feels self-serving when it's self-destructive. It's our way of controlling and catapulting ourselves into a situation that we feel is gratifying. Of course, like everything, it's about balance. Once you have balance in your life, the rest looks after itself. I believe self-harming and overeating are ways that we punish ourselves. Why are you punishing yourself? What have you done that's so bad? Who told you that you did something that bad?

Drug and alcohol addiction are the most obvious forms of "slow suicide." Through my conversations with people addicted to heroin who have ended up on the streets and wanting to kill themselves, I have heard similar stories of not being able to grieve properly in childhood. It could be for the dog that died, the goldfish that they saw washed down the drain, or a mother who wouldn't let them cry. Heroin becomes so addictive to them when they first start using, because within "heroin" lies the words "hero" and "in." I would like doctors to start understanding how therapy that focuses on allowing people to properly grieve can be used in order to help them truly heal and provide hope.

THE PERMANENT NATURE OF IMPERMANENCE

If we search for peace and harmony, we will always be disappointed. This is what the Buddha taught. The search for happiness leads only to sadness when that happiness proves to be always transient.

One of the most common themes surrounding suicide is loss – the loss of happiness, the loss of hope, or perhaps the loss of the life that someone imagined for themselves. For those left behind by suicide, there is the excruciatingly difficult loss of a loved one or friend. Remember, impermanence is the truth. What do I mean by that? Impermanence tells us that all we experience in this life is fleeting. Joy, sadness, abundance, and pain will ebb and flow.

Everything is changing, no matter how overwhelming and dark some of it may seem.

We spend a lot of time looking for enlightenment. Difficult events and circumstances present the opportunity to return from grief, loss, and sadness, back to our true enlightened state. While cherishing, servicing, and loving something or someone is wonderful and joyous, the problem arises when the time comes for change and we won't let go. We can become stuck in the cement of suffering and karma.

At a certain point in your life, something will happen that will give you the opportunity to either go deeper into the suffering, or step right back to the zero point of enlightenment. You could lose your savings, your career, even your family. Though as difficult as any situation can be – and as much as you may need to reach out for support – you have the ability to greet it with wonder. Imagine what you perceive as the worst thing that can happen to you coming to pass, then go right back to the enlightenment by saying "I wonder what's going to happen next?" There is the awe of creation in that statement, and when you say it you will have enough clarity of mind to see what happens next, and not lose the thing you need the most – hope.

Our paths are all different. What brings someone to suicide or suicidal thoughts varies, as do the ways we can deal with its urgency. There is always hope and light, even in the darkest tunnel. As much as someone tries to understand another person's feelings, ultimately there must be self-compassion. Depression especially, has a way of isolating us. Spending time on your own, or on social media (where constantly comparing yourself to others, or being bullied, is a real risk) instead of out in the world, feeds depression. Drug and alcohol use can cause even more alienation, and a cycle of self-medicating that increases the isolation. In truth, you are not alone, and staying silent about your problems will keep the door from opening to other possibilities and solutions. The same is true about helping someone in your life who is in dire need of support.

Support (in whatever form you find it), exercise, eating well, meditation, and other self-care practices can easily fall away when there's a slide toward deep depression and suicidal thoughts. Take the smallest of steps for yourself, or help someone suffering to put these tools into, or back into, their lives. Reaching out for therapy, and sometimes medication (especially in cases where you or the person is in an extremely dangerous state of mind) is so important, but no one or no thing can truly change the way you or someone who is suicidal thinks and perceives the world. There has to be a change of consciousness. The process will take the time that it needs. It may be a while before the shift is effective and lasting, but it is possible to plant the seeds of hope with reflection and communication.

Without hope we don't have anything. Life is an imperfect journey. There are steps forward and steps that take us in reverse; there are victories and obstacles. Everything has its own divine timing. Finding a way to stay hopeful is so important. It is a major driving force in life. If you lose hope, it is easy to slip into darkness. Individually and collectively, we need to bring hope to our lives through communication and recognizing what our dreams are. We should help ourselves, and others, to get as close as possible to fulfilling those dreams.

ATTITUDE IS EVERYTHING – THE WILLINGNESS TO STAY POSITIVE

We all have storms in our lives at certain times. Often these situations or events are based in lack or in fear. We experience lack of money, love, relationships, work, or many other parts of life. The fear of this lack, sometimes even before it becomes reality, can affect the way we see ourselves. Lack and fear drive so much of our unhappiness.

Your attitude determines cause and effect. To be at cause is to be empowered; to be at effect is disempowering. All that it takes to switch an attitude is willingness. If you can talk about everything that has happened in your life - tragedy, loss, and gain – in a heartfelt way, there is wisdom. You won't be able to find that wisdom or understand it if you haven't got the ability to be calm when the storm hits the present, or even when it has passed.

Many of us have experienced painful events in our lives that we carry into the present. Whatever is going on in your life, the attitude you bring to the table finds influence in the past. How each person tolerates their challenges is dependent on their coping mechanisms. What we learned in our childhood - often as a means of emotional survival - is a part of how we sink in to, or swim out of, our problems. The same events can send one person into a deep depression, while someone else will be able to move through it and let it go. Although our support systems and other circumstances play a role, attitude can be the most powerful part of the equation.

Recognizing and processing the painful things that have happened in your life is very beneficial, but at a certain point understanding that there is nothing you can do to change it historically, is true freedom from its destructive power. Your attitude is what changes. Ultimately, that is the only thing you control. It takes a true willingness to let go of emotions that, in truth, are only hurting you further. Those emotions are serving a purpose in how you choose to live. Sometimes they are keeping you "safe" from relationships, or comfortable in the role of victimhood, or not having to feel the glorious variety of life's experiences. When you stay in negativity, you are not facing your genuine self. In order to live fully, and guard against severe depression, you have to accept, let go, and look upon your "story" with a different, positive attitude that empowers you.

If you, or someone close to you, have recently experienced depression, and the phrase "I feel as if I'm slipping back," or "It seems I'm sinking deeper," are expressed, be aware that those very words, and the body language that often accompanies it, can trigger suicidal thought patterns. Recognize that slippery path. The feelings are real, but further negative thoughts can be the deciding factor in whether they take over, or are a temporary setback. This is the most dangerous time, since fear of slipping back into depression is a major cause of suicide.

I believe that our mind is creating our reality. Once we start to think in a negative way, we become negative, and when we think in a positive way, we become positive. That's why the positive suggestion industry is worth billions every year. It's about understanding that the more positive you can be in life - because you have hope and you have courage and you have strength - chances are that depression is not going to visit you for a long time. That said, everyone, at some stage in their life, is going to have depression.

There are things we can do to turn around the energy of depression. Self-care, of both the mind and the body, builds your resilience to depression and dark feelings. We create our reality, even up against circumstances that seem crushing. Learning to stay positive in the midst of challenging times is key. How we talk to, and address ourselves, is a huge factor. We truly are our own best friend – or worst enemy. If you're not in control of your mind, it's in control of you. What other people do or say is not important – it is what you think that makes a difference in your positivity about life.

Depression is low energy, in both the physical and mental aspects of your being. Exercise, creativity, and even simple human interaction act as remedies to low energy and depression. What do you do when you are too depressed to take care of yourself? Along with looking toward outside support, you can use simple tools, such as closing your eyes and imagining yourself filled with energy – maybe even rocket fuel! If you get into the habit of trying this, it will help you take that first step, which is always the hardest. Once we are moving, that becomes our new reality. Get out of your house, walk, draw, or paint. Check out a book from the library, chat with your neighbor about the weather, or go to a park – whatever it takes. Low energy can easily begin to create a chemical imbalance in your body that will lead to even lower vitality. Empower yourself by plugging your batteries into something that has more energy than you, every day.

Staying positive means taking that voice that comes from deep inside your subconscious mind – the one that says you're not good enough, or you failed, or you will never be happy – and reprogramming it. Examining where those words come from (perhaps a parent or a teacher berated you) can help you understand. It may be as simple as just lighting a candle, taking a couple of deep breaths, and allowing your body to relax. When your body relaxes, the subconscious begins to open. It's as if you are shining a torch into a dark room. If you extend that beam out, you'll see more of your mind, which is very important in order to stay positive. Life is too short to let other people, your history, or even your current circumstances tell you who you are. That isn't the definition of your truth. Your identity is independent of external forces. You are your heart, your mind, and your spirit.

The next time the negative voice starts talking to you, visualize sending it on its way. You can envelop it in a warm, loving light until it turns into beautiful energy. You can shoot a golden arrow through it. Use mini-meditations, affirmations, and other tools that work for you (a longer meditation at the end of this book is helpful for painful, negative feelings.) Speaking to yourself in a positive voice has a miraculous power – and it comes from you. Use what I call "The Three P's" - Be Positive, Be Precise, and Be Pleased. Instead of "I'm not confident," or "I am not going to be able to make this relationship work," or "I'm not going to be able to do this job successfully," speak in the positive, be precise as to what you want, and be pleased with the energy you've put into it. "I have love," "I can do this work," "I am good enough," are messages heard by your subconscious.

Reaching back to positive events and feelings in your life can be a tool to keep dark feelings from taking over. Those events offer hope by triggering positive emotions in your mind, or in the consciousness of a person that you are trying to help. A loving experience that exists in our psyche's memory can be the difference between going through with a suicide or not. Keep reminding people about how beautiful their family, their children, and nature are. Point out the amazing aspects of life. Remember what there is to cherish, every day, and you'll find it easier to weather any event – even the deaths of those we love. You will be able to hold on to a lot of joy.

Service is a great way to get out from under your own negative internal voice. The greatest help you can find for yourself is the act of helping others. Again, I will remind you that if your depression (or your loved one's depression) is persistent and worrisome, please reach out to others to address it. Try to gain perspective - if you are able - by doing something, however small, for someone else. You manifest happiness for yourself when you serve. It is your path to what is rightfully yours, and it will bring you joy. When you are in service, you're eliminating anger, jealousy, hurt, and guilt, all through the creation of compassion.

Once you make up your mind to have a positive attitude, no matter what happens in your life, you take away the power of "the storm." That's how powerful you are, that's how powerful we become together. Everything that is going on outside of you has first manifested on the inside. If things are happening in the world around you, it's because it's happening within you. If you adopt a positive attitude you will be given access to the part of the mind, which unfortunately on the planet at this time, is stronger than our conscious mind. It's called the unconscious mind. The unconscious mind controls everything. How many times have you put energy into manifesting something, and then it didn't turn out the way you wanted it to? Is that failure? There's no such thing as failure, there is only feedback. So if something else manifests than what you set out to manifest, therein lies the feedback that says there is something in your unconscious that is stronger than your conscious. It is up to you to be still and find out what that limiting belief is that is holding you back.

THE VALUE OF VULNERABILITY

Fear is an emotion that drives so much of human behavior. There is always a choice to choose love (and self-love) over fear, but we often struggle with the two. Though the root causes of suicide or suicidal thoughts are complex, fear can be a factor that pushes depression deeper. There is fear of failure, fear of relationships, fear of being alone, fear of financial insecurity – even fear of life itself. There will always be periods of challenge in our lives. The happiest people are not the ones without strife and pain, but the individuals who are most accepting of their vulnerability. They choose to embrace vulnerability, rather than fear it. That is true resilience.

No one wants to feel vulnerable to hurt and manipulation. Indeed, we must stand up for ourselves, and walk away from toxic situations. Remember though, we won't always be strong or unaffected by problems and trauma, and so much of our external world cannot be controlled. If you know you are vulnerable, yet you love yourself no matter what comes your way, you have a guard against depression. Vulnerability is strength. Being human is a fragile state. Anything can happen to us at any time. Your strength comes from your ability to remain open to all the experiences that life has for us. The goal is to get to a stage where you begin to stop tagging those events and situations as good or bad, and you just call them "experiences". Vulnerability is having the courage to be truthful and say, "I am not perfect."

Fear tries to protect you by shutting you down. Vulnerability opens you to possibility, and the likelihood of change. We can't live shielded from life's sorrows and challenges that are manifesting in the present, nor can we change the past. Memories may trigger feelings that affect the way someone perceives themselves surrounding a present-day situation. Being unemployed for a long time could call up the recollection of family financial strain, or perhaps a parent going into a deep depression. Suicide may seem like a safe place for someone whose fear of continued pain has crossed a line and is unbearable. Hopefully, there's an opening that can be found in that mindset that can allow light in. There is always the opportunity to transform fear into love. Communication is the avenue to healing.

We are greater than our fears. Though they may cause us to lose sight of who we are, the truth is that you are the creators of your own destiny. There are times when reaching out for help is the best thing we can do for ourselves. Strife and depression can be a wake-up call. If we stay in fear, it can devastate our lives. Underneath fear is anger. Many times we can trace self-hate and suicidal thoughts back to suppressed anger. Someone who thinks that dying is the only way out may have turned anger they have (from abuse or neglect) on to themselves. Whether they are killing themselves slowly, or contemplating a quick death, they have probably not recognized and processed the anger that has played such a destructive role in their lives.

Fear can worsen any physical and/or chemical issues that contribute to someone's depression. It can even manifest as fear of the actual depression (misunderstanding it, thinking there's no solution to it, feeling condemned or labeled "crazy" for being depressed.) There are people who sense they are severely depressed yet won't get help because of fear. They believe depression and mental illness come from weakness, when in truth it is just like having any other physical condition. We all have to create a world where depression is accepted and not stigmatized. If we dispensed with any negative belief around depression, it would save lives. Suicide has a lot of shame attached to it. This is one of the biggest hurdles for prevention.

Fear is a lack of faith - the faith that you are good enough, and worthy of happiness. Faith also means that whatever is meant for you will come to you no matter what you do to try to stop it. That's a hard lesson, but a true and important one. If something or someone is not meant for you, it will never come to you. Pulling it or grasping at it won't help. You have to empower yourself with the faith that we will all die someday, but that we have the ability to fill that space between birth and death with what we want and what is important to our survival - peace of mind.

OUR INNER LIFE AND OUTSIDE INFLUENCES

Depression, and other struggles that sometimes drive people to the brink, have been around for a long time, but we live in a time where there are so many new external influences. When examining the topic of suicide, it's helpful to look at how outside influences affect our inner lives. How can we understand this relationship better in order to help ourselves, and others?

There's no denying that the constant interconnectedness of the world (which is often not true human connection) through social media, technology, and other almost instantaneous modes of communication, can slant reality, empower negativity, and alienate people. Even watching too much television exposes us to heavy, negative influences that do not help the quality of our lives. You must make an active decision about your environment, the company you keep, and what you want to achieve in life. Passively soaking up destructive influences around you, and taking in information from sources that you should not give much power to, distracts you from the reality that you are whole and wonderful as you are. When you focus on your own life, you begin to create all kinds of possibilities that lift depression and feelings of hopelessness.

Social media speeds up and heightens bullying. It is a growing cause of suicide, especially amongst teens. There are many children experiencing bullying during their school years, sometimes on a regular basis. The effect on their self-image can be devastating and long lasting. When kids grow up with bullying, they lose sight of what is acceptable in how they treat one another. In the worst-case scenarios, suicidal

feelings and actions can develop. Many
people still suffer the effects of bullying that
happened long ago. It can take place between
adults – in relationships, at the workplace,
and within families. If we look not just at the
victim, but also at the bully with compassion,
we gain insights and answers. We need to
change the environment of intolerance to the
atmosphere of acceptance and recognition,
improving our world for the better. There is
hope.

If we have more positive attitudes and
feelings about ourselves, we can balance
negative external influences. No matter
what the situation or circumstances someone
finds themselves in, coming back to a
foundation of positive self-worth is the first
step in creating some resilience to hurt and
pain. If you suspect your child, friend, or
family member is experiencing bullying or
abuse, look for the signs. Have they become
withdrawn and disinterested in the things
they used to enjoy? Is there a change in

confidence? In the case of children, there may be physical marks on them. Speak up, get help, and reach out. There are anti-bullying programs in schools and organizations available to you for support.

Cyber bullying is so pervasive these days. It is probably the worst form of bullying because of how easy it has become for people to be abusive, without having to face their victims. We need to be aware and caring before it gets out of hand and leads to tragedy. Step in when someone is being bullied – compliment them, support them and take action to stop it. If you have a child who is the bully, take a long hard look at the environment that you have created while raising that child. Do you speak against certain people or use hurtful words and tones and/or gossip? We create our life and affect those around us. As mentors to our children, we influence their behavior.

Our attitude, mind, and energy all play a large part in creating our reality. That goes for the bully or abuser also. If somebody is bullying you, or your child, they probably have issues of confidence. Light a candle and say a prayer for them. They need as much help as the people who are their victims. If a bully can find the root cause of the behavior, healing is possible for everyone involved.

Depression latches on to the idea that we are different, and somehow unacceptable. Though diversity is increasingly celebrated and attitudes of tolerance seem to be changing for the better, on the smaller, everyday scale of people's lives, there are too many situations and dynamics where people are left feeling that they don't fit in. Wanting to belong is a human need, yet accepting your differences (all of them - who you are, what you like, your joys, your problems, etc.) and loving yourself, is so essential in order to cope, stave off depression, and weather all the outside influences. Of course, depression and suicidal feelings are more complicated than just ignoring a bully, or pushing away negative energy, but when we look at the big picture of how we treat one another we can manifest a more positive environment.

It is important to watch our thoughts. When we catch a feeling of self-criticism triggered by an outside influence, we can just say to ourselves, "Cancel, I send love." It is as simple as stopping in the moment. Does it mean that the feeling won't ever come back, or that we have solved the challenges that have driven our emotions to a difficult place? Probably not, but in that moment you are pausing and creating the space for new ways of thinking to flow. Changing your mood for even just a minute can instruct your mind on how to feel positive. It is a continuous process to monitor the mind, and work at continually maintaining a positive attitude about yourself and life. Sometimes it is a slow lesson, but an effective one in the end.

CHANGING YOUR BELIEFS ABOUT YOURSELF - PEACE AS A LIFESTYLE

With all the contributing factors to suicidal thought and action – both external and internal – we can feel overwhelmed by how best to help ourselves, or someone we are close to. There is an overall attitude to approaching all of life's issues, especially the most serious and urgent ones. Adopting a peaceful state of harmony as a lifestyle is a goal that can clear the way to mindfulness about all our problems and challenges. Our beliefs are our reality. By changing those beliefs, we can allow serenity and self-compassion to begin to change and transform our lives.

We have to create peace as a lifestyle ourselves, even if it means that part of your peace is knowing that you need to reach out for help. What is the difference between a peaceful and a non-peaceful manifestation? When an event happens in your life, there are only going to be two different kinds of responses – to look at it as a positive or a negative - and it's up to you to choose which one. If you experience a severe blow to your finances, your work, or your relationship, it could affect how you feel about yourself and cause you to fall into extreme sadness or anger. Alternatively, you can carry on, taking things one day at a time. There will be grief, adjustment, and struggle, but you'll be able to remember that life is a pendulum, swinging from joy to sorrow, and back again. When you lose a house, the value is the people within it, it is not the bricks and mortar. Peace as a lifestyle is the understanding that events and situations will happen. There is nothing we can do except choose to be peaceful about them and see what manifests. Everything happens for a reason; look for the positive reason.

If you feel unworthy of having good things in your life, follow that belief back to its root cause. Where does the feeling come from, and what perspective can you bring to it now? When you look at the past, don't stay there. Bring yourself back to the present. How are you right now in this moment? The past is past; how are you right here, right now? Looking at past emotions is not the same thing as feeling them all over again. Fear of the pain is what keeps so many people from being able to search within themselves, especially when it involves seeking help to do so. The first step is the willingness to live in peace. It can become a habit and an addiction to see everything negatively. You can replace the habit of chaos and unhappiness with the habit of peace.

As mentioned previously, when someone has reached the point where suicide seems like an option, or an answer, there may be a calmness that comes over them three days before an attempt. If you are feeling this way, or suspect someone in your life is, get help right away. Peace in life is knowing that there will be darkness, but accepting it, no matter how difficult. It is a process of gentle learning, and openness to teachings and support, that expand and improve our lives, along with knowing where to go for help.

SUICIDE AWARENESS – WHAT EVERYONE NEEDS TO KNOW

Each year, approximately one million people worldwide die by suicide. That is one every 40 seconds, or 3,000 per day. Twelve out of each 100,000 deaths are suicides, and that number is growing. Presently, it is the 10th leading cause of mortality. More people die of suicide than in wars. For each death there are at least 20 attempted suicides. That alarming number reminds us of the great need to address this challenging and urgent subject.

Practical actions and knowledge to prevent suicide is an important part of turning a life around – whether it is yours or a person close to you. If we can help stop the urgent hopelessness that we, or the other person, are feeling, healing can begin. (Please see the suicide hotline numbers and prevention organization's websites printed in the back of this book.)

If you are feeling suicidal, know that finding some sort of coping mechanism, however difficult it may seem, can get you to the next step where you can start to move out of the darkness. By picking up and reading this book you are already in a state of recognition, which is a large part of the journey. You must find the willingness to talk about your feelings and reach out for help. Seek out a solid, dependable support network, even if it is just one person.

When it is someone close to you who is going through a very deep depression and seemingly at risk for suicide, it can be extremely difficult and confusing to know how you can help. We understand that we need to do what we can to save a life, yet sometimes our caution, lack of confidence about "the right thing to do", and even our fear can prevent us from trying. Take the time now to learn what is possible – and necessary – to assist someone in great need.

We can get caught up in some of the misconceptions about suicide. There is a myth that once a person has decided to end their life, that we cannot talk them out of it. The truth is, if they get help there is always a chance that they will change their mind (though at a certain point they will do what they decide for themselves – we are not responsible for that.) Another false belief is people who are suicidal don't want help. Statistics show that more than 50% of people were in therapy no less than 6 months before they died. Though this may show therapy is certainly not a foolproof solution in all cases, it does speak to people in pain wanting help.

We may think a person in trouble will get angry if you try to help. Even if someone doesn't respond the way you would wish for, by opening up the lines of communication they know you are there for them. This alone might relieve some of the stress of the situation. Many people feel that if they're not a therapist, they can't help. People who are considering suicide really want to be helped but don't always know how to reach out, they want to know someone cares about them, cares if they live or die. Nothing you say can be wrong if you come from genuine love, compassion and caring. Everyone can learn ways to help either directly or by steering someone towards professional aid.

Both teens and the elderly have become more susceptible to suicide. Alienation, loneliness, and the sense of not fitting in are high amongst these groups. Teens might be struggling with their identities, and older people sometimes feel abandoned or worthless. We live in a society propelled by money and the need to pay bills. The family structures are breaking down because no one has time for one another. We need to get back to family meals and discussions. We're losing the values that give us hope and the guidelines that define our paths. If we compromise our values, we compromise society.

Stay aware of the warning signs, which typically increase the week before someone attempts, or carries out, a suicide. Never assume that if a person talks about it, that it just means they are only looking for the attention or understanding, and won't actually attempt or go through with suicide. It may be a cry for help and a release of the pressure they are under, like the steam letting off from a pressure cooker. Try to listen closely and let them know you are there.

It's my belief, because of my research and experience with many suicidal people, that some suicides are cries for help that go wrong. The person may have been attempting it as a way of reaching out, but could not control the outcome, which can lead to an accidental death. I have spoken to people that told me they nearly killed themselves, and were so shocked it turned them away from suicide as a solution to their problems.

Risk Factors

There are risk factors that can lead to suicidal feelings or attempts. Be aware of how these situations, events, and/or conditions affect you, or someone close to you that you are concerned about.

- Depression, bi-polar disease, and other mental conditions.
- Abuse of alcohol and/or drugs. Relapses after sobriety or "getting clean" can be especially difficult for the individual to cope with. Forty percent of suicide victims have alcohol in their blood levels.

- A family history of suicide.
- Previous suicide attempts.
- Medical conditions, especially ones that cause chronic, severe pain.
- High stress and/or prolonged stress.
- Ongoing verbal and/or physical abuse, or abuse in the past.
- Financial, career, school, relationship, or family problems.
- Death of spouse, child, or best friend.
- Other jarring or tragic events, which can come at the end of other challenges, leading to the feeling of "the last straw."
- Teen depression, especially if it stems from bullying or other abuse. Cyber-bullying has become a serious factor in teen suicide. Also, look for self-destructive behavior. Young people may not know they are depressed or have the knowledge and ability to express it.
- Challenges with sexuality, gender,

and identity. Young men in particular are struggling to find role models as they have become more metro-sexual, i.e. not the rough man or "man's man," that used to be the image that society expected.

- Elderly depression, coupled with extreme loneliness and/or debilitation.

Warning Signs

Some signs that a person is thinking about or planning suicide are obvious; some are not. As mentioned, it is not unusual to think your friend or loved one is doing better and that the depression has lifted, only to be followed by a suicide or an attempt. They may very well have felt good, but since it wasn't a true change in the underlying feelings about themselves, the "high" of temporary relief, like the high of a drug, came crashing down. They hit a place where hope is lost. When they settle on killing themselves, a light of peace happens and disappearing from life seems like a real option.

There is a common thread I hear with the many people I've worked with who have had suicide visit their lives - the person who died by suicide showed more obvious signs (listed below) between one to three days before the incident. If someone has a sudden turnaround of his or her depression, stay aware of what might be happening under the surface.

Here are the most common warning signs that there is a severe feeling of hopelessness, which may signify that someone is thinking of suicide:

- Isolating themselves.
- Feeling desperate and trapped, as if there is no "way out."
- Feeling hopeless with no reason to live; the inability to see anything

positive about the future.

- Feeling like a burden; expressing self-loathing.
- Saying death seems like an option.
- Expressing a plan to carry out a suicide.
- Speaking about or writing excessively about death and dying.
- Seeking medications or a gun.
- Personality changes.
- Changes in eating and sleeping (with depression).
- Getting "affairs in order" or giving away possessions.
- A very sudden calm and happiness after seeming suicidal - they have decided to follow through with the plan to die by suicide and no longer seem troubled. They feel they've settled on a solution.

When you suspect that someone may be feeling suicidal, listen closely for some of the thoughts they might communicate, either in a conversation about their feelings, or even in an offhand way:

- "I can't go on."
- " My family will be better off without me."
- "Who cares if I'm not around."
- "I just want out."
- "I won't be around much longer."
- "Soon you won't have to worry about me."

HELP AND SUPPORT FOR YOURSELF AND OTHERS

There may be fear and uncertainty as to how to help someone who is suicidal. We can think, "What if I say the wrong thing?" or "I may push them away." Turning a blind eye and remaining silent are much more worrisome. Helping others involves two things – educating yourself about suicide, and lending openness and communicating with someone in need. Don't sit back passively. If getting involved is difficult for any reason, reach out to others who may be able to act. When a person's life is at stake, doing anything that can help is better than doing nothing. TAKE IT SERIOUSLY when you see the warning signs. Remember, it is not your job to rescue them, but to keep them safe and directed towards help.

- Express concern – tell them what they have said about their feelings. (They may not be aware because they are so depressed.)
- Ask if they are considering suicide.
- Ask if they are seeing a mental health professional and/or taking medication.
- Don't plead with them or try to talk them out of it – validate their feelings, which is different than telling them they are real. Remember that suicide may not seem like a problem, rather a solution. Say you want to lend support to get help. Have resources and contacts ready.
- Don't wait to ask questions. When in doubt, act.
- If a person is resistant, keep trying to help.
- Talk to them alone or in a private

setting. Plan time to let them talk and give the person your full attention.

- Allow them to talk freely, no matter what comes up. Don't judge them or direct their thoughts.
- If you are afraid to ask them questions, find someone who can.
- Follow-up. Continue to be available for support. Check in.
- Share hope.
- Don't offer ways to fix their problems.
- Don't blame yourself. You can't help them if you are feeling guilty. Whatever they are feeling is not your fault.
- Remove any means of suicide (medication, weapons.)
- Make a plan for them that they can call you, reach out, go a to safe place.

If a suicide seems as if it could happen soon,

don't leave the suicidal person alone. Ask very pointed questions:

- "Do you have a plan, when, how?"
- "Will you let me help you get help?"
- "Will you go with me to get help?"
- "I'm on your side – we will get through this."
- "I want you to live."
- "I'm feeling concerned for you."
- "I've noticed differences in the way you are acting and I'm wondering how you are?"
- "When did you start feeling that way?"
- "Did something happen that affected your feelings?"
- "How can I best help you?"
- "You may not believe this, but the way you feel will change."
- "Though I can't know exactly how you feel, I care about you and I'm concerned."
- -   "When you feel like giving

up, hold on for a day, an hour, even a minute."

Sources of Help

Therapy – Feelings can reoccur, even with effective therapy. It's important to stay aware about the person by checking in with them.

Medication – Medications can take time, along with finding the most effective one or a combination. Sometimes medication can lead to a reaction that increases the risk of suicide, especially in teens and young adults, yet it can be helpful in many cases of severe depression. A lot of care and consideration – along with the required medical monitoring by a doctor – is important.

Drug and alcohol treatment – When someone begins to see how their substance abuse is heightening their depression, they may find hope (even if sobriety takes some time to achieve.)

In an emergency, please use suicide prevention hotlines or call the person's therapist or family. If the situation can't be helped any other way, take them to the emergency room or call the police if they refuse help and are about to hurt or kill themselves.

COPING WITH SUICIDE LOSS – GRIEF AND HEALING

Losing someone close to you to suicide is perhaps the most difficult loss there is. Even if it was clear and obvious that someone was suffering from severe depression or crushing circumstances that might identify the "why" of their death, the tremendous pain, questions, and wrenching emotions remain.

Though we can become stuck on the idea that it was a "choice" the person made to end their lives, it is somewhat helpful to try to remember that they themselves saw no choice. It may not ease the grieving process, yet the reality of what has happened is that the person was in a mindset that became their truth, whether they thought about it for a long time, or acted impulsively. They may have been getting help, or the suicide might have seemed to come from nowhere. As mentioned, it might have even been an accident, in that they were crying out for help by attempting suicide and thought they wouldn't actually die. Whatever the cause was, the suicide victim did not see any other way out of their pain except to end, or attempt to end, their life.

A death by suicide is an extremely complicated experience for survivors. So many emotions arise: shock, devastating sadness, guilt, anger, and abandonment – often felt all at the same time. There is not a specific roadmap for what someone goes through after a suicide of someone close to them, but here's a common path:

Shock – The feeling of numbness and disorientation. This stage can actually be protective, since the sadness may be overwhelming if felt all at once.

Denial – This can happen when the numbness wears off and feelings arise that you are not ready to accept. You might begin to tell yourself and others that you are fine, when in reality you are still in the early part of the grieving process. Be patient with yourself and allow yourself to be vulnerable.

Guilt – Suicide brings an onslaught of guilt for those close to the person who died. The feeling can range from "I should have known," "I didn't do enough to help them," or "If only I had done something differently." Parents and spouses are especially subject to the crushing helplessness of guilt. Remember that no one can affect or control another person's ability to cope. Blaming ourselves keeps us from accepting that truth. It is not possible for you to change another person or their thoughts; they have to do it themselves. Once somebody makes a decision to follow through with a suicide, they are responsible for their actions. Nothing you do will change the outcome if the help and support offered to the person has no effect. What you can do is make the valued effort now, while people are alive, to communicate with them, befriend them, and care about them. If they go ahead with suicide, you will know you did all that was possible, and that you had a great relationship while they were here.

Sadness – This is a natural and predictable effect of suicide. Using coping skills, getting help, talking about it, all help move towards acceptance and some lessening of grief. It's true that things have changed now, that must be mourned. Time will help but know that the scar will always be there, but you must find a way to make peace with it.

Anger – Though it may seem counter productive or even cruel to feel anger at someone who has died by suicide, exploring those feelings are essential. Reminding yourself that the depression or circumstances that led to the suicide may have made it impossible for them to think about the hurt they would cause if they died by suicide, can help. No matter how much pain you knew they were in, you will still probably experience some anger. It could be a step toward understanding how you feel as a survivor and coming to a place of acceptance.

Acceptance – As you move through the intense feelings surrounding suicide, you can ultimately find a way to accept – not forget – the loss. Whereas we may feel we could not go on at the onset of the news, we learn to find how to heal, and what our natural rhythm of that healing will be. Above all else, someone who has lost a loved one to suicide must be gentle and loving to themselves.

If you or someone you know has been touched by suicide loss, please know there is support and help available in many different forms. Individual or family therapy, support groups (some with a very specific focus, for example, coping with military suicide or teen suicide,) and organizational outreach programs, are all within reach. There are books and materials, and often, with time, ways to volunteer or get involved in awareness and prevention. Some survivors find this outlet helpful in their grieving process, as well as a way to honor the person they lost.

What are some of the coping tools for those left behind?

- Try not to isolate. Reach out to people who care about you and in whom you can find comfort in. Spend time with friends and family who can listen. Have people you can call when you need to.
- Don't feel that you must show strength or any other specific emotion. All your feelings are valid. Your grieving process must follow its own timetable. There is no right

way or schedule.

- You are more prone to depression when you experience this kind of loss, even years down the line. It's important to stay aware of your feelings and seek help when needed. Don't go it alone when it feels like more than a passing emotion.

- You may experience some lessening of the pain for a spell, then suddenly feel triggered by something, and fall into extreme sadness. Know that there will be setbacks.

If you are trying to help a friend who is processing the loss, offer support in the way of providing food and/or childcare, running errands, or any other task that can alleviate responsibilities. Relieve the person of some of their everyday duties and obligations while they are going through this difficult period. Don't be afraid of saying the wrong thing, or not knowing what to express. This feeling can drive you away, and the person who has experienced the loss may not understand. Even the words "I am so sorry, I wish I knew what to say," can be huge. Your friend knows that you don't hold the answers or have the ability to make the pain disappear.

HEALING FROM PAIN – A MEDITATION

Whichever way suicide is playing a role in your life – through your own feelings and ability to cope, or by assisting someone in crisis, or if you are trying to pick up the pieces after a death by suicide – a meditation, along with other supportive healing outlets and therapies, can help tremendously. Some tools are simple, such as the practice of looking up and to the right – where goodness and peace will come to you - when you are feeling sad. If you look down and to your left, you create beta-blockers and depression.

The meditation that follows can help you find peace inside yourself, and with the world around you. Emotional pain serves as a message to stop, slow down, and look at the source of the hurt. Pain can obscure the reality that everything is changing all the time. Nothing is permanent. Though suffering will visit us time and again, knowing that the continuum of life is part of being alive reminds us that life is, indeed, worth living. When you clear the mind, you achieve a better sense of perspective about who you are, what you need, and how best to practice self-care. Self-care also means the ability to reach out to others for help if you need it.

Find a quiet place where you won't be disturbed and make yourself as comfortable as possible. Take two or three deep breaths. As you exhale on the third breath, close your eyes, relax, and let go. Switch off the world for the next ten to fifteen minutes.

Allow your mind to settle into a space of peace. Imagine that there is a gold orb of bright light – like a setting or rising sun - over your head. Feel its warmth. Picture the gold orb slowly drifting into your mind and resting there. After a while, it flows down from your head into your neck and throat, then begins to spread across your shoulders. The golden light feels warm and healing, eliminating any stress you are feeling.

Imagine the light rolling down your shoulders and into your arms, gently caressing, healing, smoothing, and relaxing all of your being. Feel it move into your elbows, forearms, wrists, hands, and fingers. From your shoulders, it begins to seep into your chest, eliminating the stress. The light now drifts down into your abdomen, comforting, calming, and caring for you. The warmth flows from your hips into the tops of your legs, and then from your legs down to your knees. Take your time to let it envelop you. There's no rush. Let the light gently drift at its own pace, like honey dripping off a spoon.

Picture the light moving down your shins and calves into your ankles, then through your feet and toes. Think of the ground beneath you. The light is flowing through your being into Mother Earth. It carries away any fears, anxieties, or hurts that you may have experienced in your life, and transforms them into love and light. As you continue to sit quiet, calm, and relaxed, imagine that two angels have just come and stood behind you. Think of them as guardian angels and trust that they are there, even if you have a hard time picturing what they look like. Ask for their help and guidance with the issues in your life. Know that these angels have, and always will be, around us, showing up from time to time in our lives as other beings. They may show up as people who care for us, or as friends. Imagine that these angels are asking the universe to allow you to feel at peace with yourself. Now, each of these angels begins to send gold light from their heart to your heart, taking away any sadness, fear, resentments, or disappointments that you may have experienced. Feel the weight of these emotions lifted off of your being.

In this state, you will come into a knowing and wise place that has always existed inside of you, previously concealed by pain. From this consciousness you can begin to apply the teaching that the best way to end trouble is to send love. If you are able, imagine that gold light moving from your heart to the people, situations, and experiences that you need to acknowledge or change. Let the light flow from you to them. If you find it difficult to send this loving gold light at this time, imagine the two angels are sending it for you on your behalf. Send it to people who might have hurt you in the past, people who don't understand you, and send it forward to everyone, knowing that it will be there in the future when you need someone to help you. Send the loving light to the past, the present, the future - and all the people and situations that those times hold. Sit with this feeling of love and peace for a while, and then slowly open your eyes.

They say that which you want the most you must give away. The teaching that springs from that idea tells you if you are searching for love, you must give love away. If you are looking for wealth, you must give wealth away. By releasing them you energize the circle of light, and that circle of light will always return to its source. What you give out is what you receive. When you sit in this meditation, remember that we can send peace and love to all beings in this world that are afraid or hurting. They can experience the happiness of oneness, the happiness that brings us together to learn from each other. When we come together we learn much more deeply than when we're alone.

Try to take some time out every day for meditation. If you have limited time, just sitting peacefully, lighting a candle, and watching it for five minutes can be of huge benefit to your overall well-being. We should always try to give ourselves something that costs nothing, and this is it!

When you want to gain deeper insight about issues and problems in your life, sit still, close your eyes, then offer the question. Remain still, and let the quiet clarity come to you. You have an amazing amount of wisdom built into your own system and psyche. Bliss lives within you. Know that part of that wisdom is also the ability to reach out for help when you need it. Allow yourself to be valued and cared for. No matter what your problems or challenges, you are part of a loving universe.

USA National Suicide Prevention Lifeline
1-800-273-TALK (8255)
http://www.afsp.org

UK Suicide Hotline +44 (0) 8457 90 90 90

Ireland Suicide Hotline 1850 60 90 90

ABOUT THE AUTHOR

For more than 20 years, Derek O'Neill has been transforming the lives of thousands of people around the world for the better. An internationally acclaimed transformational coach and therapist, motivational speaker, author, martial arts sensei and humanitarian, Derek inspires and uplifts people from all walks of life through his workshops, consultations, speaking engagements, media, and tireless humanitarian work.

Drawing on thirty years of training in martial arts, which earned him the level of Master Black Belt, coupled with his extraordinary intuitive abilities and expertise as a psychotherapist, Derek has pioneered a new psychology, transformational therapy. His signature process, aptly named "The Sword and the Brush," helps clients to seamlessly transmute their struggles into positive outcomes, using the sword to cut away old patterns and the brush to help paint the picture of the new life that they require.

In addition to reaching large audiences through workshops and media, Derek advises individuals, celebrities, business leaders, and politicians, helping them to find new perspectives on long-standing issues and bringing harmony back to their lives and businesses.

Author of More Truth Will Set You Free, the Get a Grip series of pocket books, a cutting edge book on parenting titled Calm Mama,

Happy Baby, and several children's books, Derek also hosted his own radio show, "The Way With Derek O'Neill," which enjoyed the most successful launch in VoiceAmerica's history, quickly garnering 100,000 listeners.

Derek is a master at offering practical wisdom and proven techniques for living a more harmonious and fulfilling life, bringing CEOs to the level of wise yogi and wise yogis to CEO; he has worked with executives from some of the world's major airlines, and the cast of Spiderman on Broadway to help transform group disharmony and untapped creative potential into productivity and dynamic performance. He has been featured in Exceptional People Magazine, The Irish Independent, The Irish Examiner, CBS television, and RTE, Ireland's national TV network.

Inspired by his worldly travels, he formed SQ Foundation, a not-for-profit organization focused on helping to solve global issues facing humanity today. In 2012, he was honored as Humanitarian of the Year and named International Celebrity Ambassador for Variety International the Children's Charity. He was welcomed as Vice President of the esteemed charity in May 2013.

Recordings of Derek's discourses are available for download, offering practical wisdom and proven techniques for living a more harmonious and fulfilling life.

To learn more about Derek O'Neill, to attend his next workshops, to order books, downloads, video streaming, or to contact him, please visit his website:

www.derekoneill.com

To learn more about **SQ Foundation**, the global charity that is changing the lives of hundreds of thousands of people around the world, go to:

www.sq-foundation.org

MORE RESOURCES FROM DEREK O'NEILL

Teachings, Books, Blog and more at
derekoneill.com

Books
Calm Mama, Happy Baby

Get a Grip Book Series
Happiness - You Must Be Effin' Joking!
Anger – Who Gives a Shite?
Relationships – Would You Want to Date You?
Depression – What's that?
Weight – What's Eating You?
Confidence – Easy for You to Say
Abundance – Starts Right Now
Fear - A Powerful Illusion
Addiction - What a Cover-Up!
Excellence - You Never Lost It, You Forgot It
Grief - Mind Boggling, but Natural
Suicide - Fast or Slow

Children's Books
Water Drop Coloring Book
The Adventures of Lucinda in Love-Filled Fairyland

SOCIAL MEDIA

YouTube
www.youtube.com/user/DerekONeill101

Facebook
www.facebook.com/derekoneill101

Twitter
www.twitter.com/DerekONeill101
LinkedIn
www.linkedin.com/in/derekoneill101